he's just
not that
into you

Your Daily Wake-up Call

GREG BEHRENDT & LIZ TUCCILLO

he's just not that into you

Your Daily Wake-up Call

HarperElement
An Imprint of HarperCollins*Publishers*
77–85 Fulham Palace Road,
Hammersmith, London W6 8JB

The website address is: www.thorsonselement.com

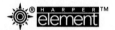

and *HarperElement* are trademarks of
HarperCollins*Publishers* Ltd

Abridged edition first published in the US
by Simon & Schuster 2005
This UK edition published by HarperElement 2006

1 3 5 7 9 10 8 6 4 2

A catalogue record of this book is
available from the British Library

ISBN-13   978-0-00-722927-7
ISBN-10   0-00-722927-5

Printed and bound in Germany by
GGP Media GmbH

This book is dedicated to all the lovely ladies out there whose stories inspired us to write this book.

May we never need to write another one.

1

If a (sane) guy really likes you, there ain't nothing that's going to get in his way. And if he's not sane, why would you want him?

2

All these years I'd been complaining
about men and their mixed messages;
now I saw they weren't mixed messages
at all. I was the one that was mixed up.

3

Knowledge is power, and more importantly, knowledge saves us time.

4

We were all beautiful, smart, funny women, and we shouldn't be wasting our time figuring out why a guy isn't calling us.

5

We're taught that in life, we should try to look on the bright side, to be optimistic. Not in this case. In this case, look on the dark side. Assume rejection first. Assume you're the rule, not the exception. It's intoxicatingly liberating.

6

We go out with someone, we get excited about them, and then they do something that mildly disappoints us. Then they keep doing a lot more things that disappoint us. Then we go into hyper-excuse mode for weeks or possibly months, because the last thing we want to think is that this great man that we are so excited about is in the process of turning into a creep. We try to come up with some explanation for why they're behaving that way, any explanation, no matter how ridiculous, than the one explanation that's the truth: He's just not that into me.

7

If the guy you're dating doesn't seem to be completely into you, or you feel the need to start "figuring him out," please consider the glorious thought that he might just not be that into you. And then free yourself to go find the one that is.

8

Wasting time with the wrong person is just time wasted. And when you do move on and find your right person, believe me, you're not going to wish you had gotten to spend more time with Stinky the Time-Waster or Freddy Can't-Remember-to-Call.

9

When a guy is into you, he lets you know it. He calls, he shows up, he wants to meet your friends, he can't keep his eyes or hands off of you, and when it's time to have sex, he's more than over-joyed to oblige.

10

Men are not complicated, although we'd like you to think we are.

11

If a dude isn't calling you when he says he will, or making sure you know that he's dating you, then you already have your answer. Stop making excuses for him; his actions are screaming the truth: He's just not that into you.

12

Move on, sister! Cut your losses and don't waste your time. Why stay in some weird dating limbo when you can move on to what will surely be better territory?

13

You know you deserve to have a great relationship.

14

Don't waste the pretty!

15

I know that guy you're dating.

He is a man made up entirely of your excuses. And the minute you stop making excuses for him, he will completely disappear from your life.

16

Are there men who are too busy or have been through something so horrible that it makes it hard for them to get involved? Yes, but there are so few of them that they should be considered urban legends.

17

A man would rather be trampled by elephants that are on fire than tell you that he's just not that into you.

18

People are inspired to do remarkable things to find and be with the one they love. Big movies are made about it, and every relationship you admire bursts with a greatness that you hope for in your own life. And the more you value yourself, the more chance you'll have of getting it.

19

You're worth it.

20

He's just not that into you if he's not asking you out. Because if he likes you, trust me, he will ask you out.

21

Men find it very satisfying to get what
they want.

22

If we want you, we will find you. If you don't think you gave him enough time to notice you, take the time it took you to notice him and divide it by half.

23

The "Maybe He Doesn't Want to Ruin the Friendship" Excuse

Here's the truth: Guys don't mind messing up a friendship if it could lead to sex, whether it be a "fuck buddy" situation or a meaningful romance.

24

I hate to tell you, but that whole "I don't want to ruin the friendship" excuse is a racket. It works so well because it seems so wise. Sex *could* mess up a friendship. Unfortunately, in the entire history of mankind, that excuse has never ever been used by someone who actually means it.

25

The "Maybe He's Intimidated by Me" Excuse

Let me say it again. Sexual harassment rules and workplace memos notwithstanding, a guy will ask out a woman of higher status if he's into her.

26

The "Maybe He Wants to Take it Slow" Excuse

If a guy truly likes you, but for personal reasons he needs to take things slow, *he will let you know that immediately*. He won't keep you guessing, because he'll want to make sure you don't get frustrated and go away.

27

The "But He Gave Me His Number" Excuse

"Give me a call." "E-mail me." "Tell Joey we should all hang out sometime." *Don't let him trick you into asking him out.* When men want you, they do the work. I know it sounds old school, but when men like women, they ask them out.

28

The "Maybe He Forgot to Remember Me" Excuse

Have faith. You made an impression. Leave it at that. If he likes you, he'll still remember you after the tsunami, flood, or Red Sox loss. If he doesn't, he's not worth your time.

29

The "Maybe I Don't Want to Play Games" Excuse

Men, for the most part, like to pursue women. We like not knowing if we can catch you. We feel rewarded when we do. Especially when the chase is a long one. We know there was a sexual revolution. (We loved it.) We know women are capable of running governments, heading multinational corporations, and raising loving children—sometimes all at the same time. That, however, doesn't make *men* different.

30

Imagine right now that I'm leaping up and down and shaking my fist at the sky. I'm on my knees pleading with you. I'm saying this in a loud voice: "Please, if you can trust one thing I say in this book, let it be this: *When it comes to men, deal with us as we are, not how you'd like us to be.*"

31

I know it's an infuriating concept—that men like to chase and you have to let us chase you. I know. It's insulting. It's frustrating. It's unfortunately the truth. My belief is that if you have to be the aggressor, if you have to pursue, if you have to do the asking out, nine times out of ten, he's just not that into you.

32

You, the superfox reading this book, are worth asking out.

33

If the men are asking you out, if the men have to get your attention, then you, in fact, are the one in control.

34

We don't need to scheme and plot and beg to get someone to ask us out. We're fantastic.

35

We did an incredibly unscientific poll where we polled twenty of our male friends (ranging from ages twenty-six to forty-five) who are in serious long-term relationships. Not one of their relationships started with the woman asking them out first. One guy even said that if she had, "It would have spoiled all the fun."

36

An excuse is a polite rejection. Men are not afraid of "ruining the friendship."

37

Don't get tricked into asking him out. If he likes you, he'll do the asking.

38

If you can find him, then he can find you. If he wants to find you, he will.

39

Just because you like to lead doesn't mean he wants to dance. Some traditions are born of nature and last through time for a reason.

40

"Hey, let's meet at so-and-so's party/any bar/friend's house" is not a date. Even if you live in New York.

41

Men don't forget how much they like you. So put down the phone.

42

You are good enough to be asked out.

43

He's just not that into you if he's not calling you. Men know how to use the phone.

44

Oh sure, they say they're busy. They say that they didn't have even a moment in their insanely busy day to pick up the phone. It was just *that crazy*. Bullshit. With the advent of cell phones and speed dialing it is almost impossible *not* to call you.

45

If I were into you, you would be the bright spot in my horribly busy day. Which would be a day when I would never be too busy to call you.

46

The "But He's Been Traveling a Lot" Excuse

For the record, a man who likes you wants to spend time with you. And he'll only settle for talking to you on the phone five times a day when he physically can't get on a plane to come see you.

47

The "But He's Got a Lot on His Mind" Excuse

When you like someone, they don't just slip your mind.

48

The big question here is, "Is it okay for a guy to forget to call me?" I'm saying to you, "No." Barring disaster—someone had to be rushed to the hospital, he was just fired from his job, someone keyed his Ferrari (kidding)—he should never forget to call you. If I like you, I don't forget you, ever. *Don't you want the guy who'll forget about all the other things in his life before he forgets about you?*

49

The "He Just Says Things He Doesn't Mean" Excuse

Most guys will say what they think you want to hear at the end of a date or a phone call, rather than nothing at all. Some guys are lying, some guys really mean it. Here's how you can tell the difference: *You know they mean it when they actually do what they said they were going to do.*

50

Here's something else to think about:

Calling when you say you're going to is the very first brick in the house you are building of love and trust. If he can't lay this one stupid brick down, you ain't never gonna have a house, baby. And it's cold outside.

51

So if a guy you're dating doesn't call when he says he's going to, why should that be such a big deal? Because you should be dating a man who's at least as good as his word.

52

The "Maybe We're Just Different" Excuse

Missing someone is a sign of a healthy relationship. Not respecting your need to have some form of connection with him while he's away is not. Regardless of his dislike for talking on the phone, he should respect and care for you enough to call you, if only because he knows that it will make you happy.

53

Is a phone call just a phone call, or is it really the almighty representation of how much he really cares about you? Probably somewhere in the middle. And a good man will know that and use this handy telecommunication device accordingly. E-mails need not apply.

54

The "But He's Very Important" Excuse

"Totally important" is another way to say "you're unimportant."

55

The word "busy" is the relationship Weapon of Mass Destruction. It seems like a good excuse, but in fact, in every silo you uncover, all you're going to find is a man who didn't care enough to call. Remember: Men are never too busy to get what they want.

56

Meeting someone you like and dating him is supposed to make you feel better, not worse. That's always a good rule to live by, no matter what the special circumstances (i.e., excuses) are.

57

The next incredible guy we meet with the really good excuse is just another guy who's hurting our feelings.

58

One hundred percent of men polled said they've never been too busy to call a woman they were really into. As one fine man said, "A man has got to have his priorities."

59

If he's not calling you, it's because you are not on his mind.

60

If he creates expectations for you, and then doesn't follow through on little things, he will do the same for big things. Be aware of this and realize that he's okay with disappointing you.

61

Don't be with someone who doesn't do what they say they're going to do.

62

If he's choosing not to make a simple effort that would put you at ease and bring harmony to a recurring fight, then he doesn't respect your feelings and needs.

63

"Busy" is another word for "asshole." "Asshole" is another word for the guy you're dating.

64

You deserve a fucking phone call.

65

He's just not that into you if he's not dating you. "Hanging out" is not dating.

66

Oh, there seem to be so many variations to dating, particularly in the early stages of a relationship. So many gray, murky areas of vagueness, mystery, and no questions asked. Dudes love this time because that's when they get to pretend they're not really dating you. Then they also get to pretend they're not really responsible for your feelings.

67

When you ask someone out on a real bonafide date, you're making it official: I'd like to see you alone to find out if we have a romantic future together (or at least pretend to listen to you while I ponder whether you're wearing a thong).

68

The "He Just Got Out of a Relationship" Excuse

He will always be able to play the "friend" card with you. He only has to be responsible for the expectations of a friend, rather than the far greater expectations of a boyfriend. After all, being a "pal," you wouldn't want to put him through any more emotional turmoil while he's going through his "very traumatic breakup." He's got the ultimate situation: a great friend with all the benefits of a girlfriend, whom he can see or not see whenever he wants to.

69

Beware of the word "friend." It can often be used by men or the women that love them to excuse the most unfriendly behavior. Personally, when I'm picking friends, I like the ones who don't make me cry myself to sleep.

70

The "But We Really Are Dating" Excuse

Men, just like women, want to feel emotionally protected when a relationship starts to become serious. One way they do that is by laying claim to it. They actually want to say "I'm your boyfriend" or "I'd like to be your boyfriend" or "If you ever break up with that other guy who's not your boyfriend, I'd like to be your boyfriend." A man who's really into you is going to want you all to himself. And why wouldn't he, hot stuff?

71

The "It's Better Than Nothing" Excuse

Really? Is better than nothing what we're going for now? I was hoping for at least a lot better than nothing. Or perhaps even something. Have you lost your marbles? Why should you feel honored for getting scraps of his time? Just because he's busy doesn't make him more valuable. "Busy" does not mean "better."

72

It's about the guy who wants you, calls you, makes you feel sexy and desired fully. He wants to see you more and more often because every time he sees you, he likes and then loves you more and more.

73

I know. Every two weeks, once a month, seeing someone, having a little love and affection may help you get through the day or the week or the month—but will it help you get through a lifetime?

74

The "But He's Out of Town a Lot" Excuse

There are ways to travel and be in a relationship, and there are ways to travel and make sure you stay out of one. The easy way to know the difference is if the guy tells you all the time how bummed he is that he has to keep leaving you. If he is not making a serious effort to make sure that while he's out of town you don't go out and find someone else, then I think you've just boarded the he's-just-not-that-into-you jet. Buckle up.

75

You have every right to know what's going on between you and someone you're knocking socks with. And the more confident you are that you deserve that (and much more), the more you'll be able to ask your big questions in a way that won't feel heavy and dramatic, I guarantee you.

76

From this moment on, right now, as you read this, make this solemn vow about your future romantic relationships: no more murky, no more gray, no more unidentified, and no more undeclared. And if at all possible, try to know someone as best you can before you get naked with them.

77

I don't want to be "sort of dating" someone. I don't want to be "kinda hanging out" with someone. I don't want to spend a lot of energy suppressing all my feelings so I appear uninvolved. I want to be involved. I want to be sleeping with someone I know I'll see again because they've already demonstrated to me that they're trustworthy and honorable—and into me.

78

Sure, in the beginning you have to be somewhat cautious about how much you give away. But that caution shouldn't be to make *them* feel more comfortable; it should be because you know that you are ultimately a delicate, valuable creature who should be careful and discerning about who gets your affection.

79

One hundred percent of guys polled said "a fear of intimacy" has never stopped them from getting into a relationship. One guy even remarked, "Fear of intimacy is an urban myth." Another guy said, "That's just what we say to girls when we're just not that into them."

80

Guys tell you how they feel even if you refuse to listen or believe them. "I don't want to be in a serious relationship" truly means "I don't want to be in a serious relationship with you" or "I'm not sure that you're the one." (Sorry.)

81

Better than nothing is not good enough
for you!

82

If you don't know where the relationship is going, it's okay to pull over and ask.

83

Murky? Not good.

84

There's a guy out there who will want to tell everyone that he's your boyfriend. Quit goofing around and go find him.

85

He's just not that into you if he's not
having sex with you. When men like
you, they want to touch you, always.

86

Ladies, you are going to meet, and have already met, many, many men in the years that constitute your dating lifespan. And I hate to tell you this, but some of these men will simply not be attracted to you. I know you're hot, but that's just the way it is. And every single one of these men that are not attracted to you will *never ever tell you that*.

87

If he were into you, he would be having a hard time keeping his paws off you. Oh, the simplicity of it all! If a man is not trying to undress you, he's not into you.

88

The "He's Afraid to Get Hurt Again" Excuse

If he were in love with you, he wouldn't be able to help himself from getting involved in a romantic relationship regardless of his fear or past experiences.

89

There are lots of reasons a man might not want to take a friendship to the "next level." It really doesn't matter what they are or if they make any sense to you. The bottom line is that when he imagines being with you more intimately (and trust me, we do think about these things), he pauses and then says to himself, "Nah." Don't spend any more time thinking about it, other than saying to yourself, "His loss."

90

The "He's So Into Me That Now He's Not" Excuse

Ahh, here comes the big "fear of intimacy" debate. Is there such a thing? Many, many people are in therapy for it, a lot of self-help books are dedicated to it, a lot of shitty behavior is excused because of it. Sure, many people have been hurt in their past, and now have a fear of intimacy. But guess what? If a man is really into you, nothing will stop him from being with you—including a fear of intimacy. He may run and get his butt into therapy if there's some serious problem, but he'll never keep you in the dark.

91

The "But it Still Feels So Good" Excuse

I know it's nice to have companionship and wake up with somebody that you really like, but that's what pets are for. Pets are God's way of saying, "Don't lower the bar because you're lonely."

92

The old-fashioned idea is that women withhold sex when they want power. It seems like men can play that game too. Why buy the cow when you can get the intimacy for free?

93

The "Multiple Excuses" Excuse

You can accept his excuses all you want, but you have to ask yourself, is this the relationship you want to be in? He may be into you, he may not, but the only thing you have to answer is, is this how you want to feel, perhaps forever?

94

One of the great joys in life is that you get to have sex. The last person who should be stopping you from enjoying that is the person you're dating.

95

Learn it, live it, like it, love it: If a man likes you, he's going to want to have sex with you. Sure, things may slow down in a long-term relationship, but even then, it's a joy, a gift, and your right to have a fantastic sex life.

96

We deserve more than a slumber party.

97

Don't ask me how I know, because I don't want to tell you, but I can assure you that my parents, who are in their seventies, after children, illnesses, aging, stressful jobs, and daily annoyances (read: life), are still having sex. If my parents can do it, so can you and your boyfriend.

98

Twenty out of the twenty men polled said, without hesitation (well, it was all done by e-mail, but they all seemed really sure about it), that they have never been really into a woman who they didn't want to have sex with. One man wrote in, "What?! Excuse me?! And the point is?!"

99

People tell you who they are all the time. When a man says he can't be monogamous, you should believe him.

100

Companionship is wonderful, but companionship with sex is even better. Call a spade a spade or, more fittingly, a friend a friend, and go find yourself a friend that can't keep his hands off you.

101

Your lost self-esteem may take longer to find than a new boyfriend, so prioritize accordingly.

102

If you're tempted to spend countless nights just cuddling with someone, buy a puppy.

103

There's someone out there that does want to have sex with you, hot stuff.

104

He's just not that into you if he's having sex with someone else. There's never going to be a good excuse for cheating.

105

Whatever problems you may have been having in your relationship, they didn't merit his having sex with someone else. Don't ask what you did wrong. Don't share the blame.

106

And in case he tells you that it just "happened," please remember, cheating doesn't just "happen." It's not an accident as in, "Oops, I just slipped and fell into a sexual relationship with someone else." It was planned and executed with the full knowledge that it could end your relationship.

107

If he's sleeping with someone else without your knowledge or encouragement, he is not only behaving like a man who's just not that into you, he's behaving like a man who doesn't even like you all that much.

108

The "He's Got No Excuse and He's Knows it" Excuse

Do all his apologies count for something? Well, you can choose to believe he is sorry. You can choose to believe he will change. But in my book, lying, cheating, or hiding is the exact opposite of the behavior of a man who's really into you.

109

Cheating is bad. Not knowing why you cheated is even worse. If one red flag isn't enough for you, how about two? Don't date any man who doesn't know why he does things.

110

The "But I've Gotten Fat" Excuse

I definitely think you should lose 175 pounds—in the form of your loser boyfriend.

His using your weight as an excuse for cheating is not only mean, but simply not valid. If he has a problem with anything in your relationship, he's supposed to talk to you about it, not put-his-penis-in-a-strange-vagina about it.

111

The "He Has a Stronger Sex Drive Than I" Excuse

There are so many ways to deal with the truly common problem of differing sex drives within a relationship. Usually one would start with an adult conversation wherein a discussion ensues that hopefully resolves with the two parties agreeing to work on it—not his jumping in the sack with *someone you know*!

112

If something is wrong in a relationship, here's a bright, mature idea: Talk about it. Don't let any man blame you for his infidelity. Ever.

113

The "But at Least He Knew Her" Excuse

You can't blame a guy for having feelings. You love someone, you break up, you still have feelings. Thank God for that, really. But having feelings doesn't mean you have to have sex.

114

If you are in a mutually established monogamous relationship, then when someone cheats on you, they have decided to blatantly disrespect a very important decision you two made together.

115

Let's call cheating what it is: a complete betrayal of trust.

116

Cheaters are people who have a lot of stuff to work out, and they're working it out on your time and with your heart.

117

Some cheaters might give you an excuse, some might not have one at all, some might even blame you. No one can tell you exactly what to do when faced with this very complicated and painful situation. But the bottom line is, is this what you had hoped for in a relationship?

118

One hundred percent of guys polled said they have never accidentally slept with anyone. (But many of them wanted to know how this accident could occur, and how they can get involved in such an accident.)

119

There is no excuse for cheating. Let me say it again. There is no excuse for cheating. Now you say it. There is no excuse for cheating.

120

Your only responsibility in someone else's lapse in judgment is to yourself.

121

Cheating is cheating. It doesn't matter whom it was with or how many times it happened.

122

Cheating gets easier every time it's done. It's only hard the first time, when one feels the sting of morality and the guilt of betraying someone's trust.

123

Cheaters never prosper. (Because they suck.)

124

A cheater only cheats himself, because he doesn't get to be with *you*.

125

Here are our five suggestions on what your man could have done if he was unsatisfied in your relationship. (You'll notice, none of them include sleeping with someone else.)

1. Talk about it.
2. Write about it.
3. Sing about it.
4. E-mail about it.
5. Even put on a puppet show about it.

126

He's just not that into you if he only wants to see you when he's drunk. If he likes you, he'll want to see you when his judgment isn't impaired.

127

Being drunk or high is an altered state that can actually take you away from real feelings. Be aware that if Boozy the Clown has to slip on the red nose every time things get intimate, it could be symptomatic of a bigger problem.

128

The "But I Like Him This Way" Excuse

You can't believe everything a guy says when he's drunk. And take it from a former bad boy: "Bad Boys" are bad because they're troubled, as in having little self-respect, lots of pent-up anger, loads of self-loathing, complete lack of faith in any kind of loving relationship, but yes, really cool clothes and often a great car.

129

Ladies, don't let your desire to be loved and feel affection cloud your judgment (like a big tall glass of scotch).

130

Know you deserve not just an affectionate, attentive boyfriend, but you deserve
an affectionate, attentive, sober one.

• 131 •

The "At Least it's Not the Hard Stuff" Excuse

Don't be fooled. Don't let the guy who's not falling down drunk and peeing in his pants get away with the fact that he is quietly, more gracefully, bombed out of his mind every single moment he's with you. It's still inebriation, it's still checking out, and it's still not good enough for you.

132

Sometimes life is incredibly difficult and painful. If you're looking for a partner to share your life with, it's better to pick someone who's able to meet it headlong with his full faculties.

133

One hundred percent of men polled said they have never vomited in the bed of a woman they were really into. (Apparently these guys don't know how to have a good time.)

134

It doesn't count unless he says it when he's sober. An "I Love You" (or any semblance thereof) while under the influence of anything stronger than grape juice won't hold up in court or in life.

135

Drinking and drug use are not a path to one's innermost feelings. Otherwise people wouldn't smash empty beer cans against their skulls or stick their fingers in fire to see if they can feel anything.

136

If he only wants to see you, talk to you, have sex with you, etc., when he's inebriated, it ain't love—it's sport.

137

Bad boys are actually bad.

138

You deserve to be with someone who doesn't have to get loaded to be around you.

139

He's just not that into you if he doesn't want to marry you. Love cures commitmentphobia.

140

Every man you have ever dated who has said he doesn't want to get married or doesn't believe in marriage, or has "issues" with marriage, will, rest assured, someday be married. It just will never be to you. Because he's not really saying he doesn't want to get married. He's saying he doesn't want to get married *to you*.

141

There is nothing wrong with wanting to get married. You shouldn't feel ashamed, needy, or "unliberated" for wanting that. So make sure from the start that you pick a guy who shares your views for the future, and if not, move on as quickly as you can. Big plans require big action.

142

The "Things Are Really Tight Now" Excuse

There will never be a good time, financially, to get married, unless you're Shaq or Ray Romano. But somehow people manage. If your man is using money as an excuse not to marry you, it's your relationship that's insecure, not his bank account.

143

You are allowed to have aspirations for your future and to know whether the relationship you're in is going to take you closer to those aspirations or be the demise of them.

144

I personally think if you have to sit and figure out what's the best way to bring up the idea of marriage to someone whom you have been intimate with for a substantial amount of time, it's not good news.

145

Most guys, or let's say the guys I want you to be dating, will make sure, as soon as reasonably possible, that you know they mean business.

146

Okay, this may be controversial, but I'm going to say it. No matter how traumatic a divorce was (and I know they can be traumatic in epic proportions), the person you plan on spending your life and having children with should love you enough to get over it if getting married is important to you.

147

Only you can decide if marriage is a deal breaker for you.

148

Marriage is a tradition that has been somewhat imposed on us, and therefore has a lot of critics. Be that as it may, if someone is as against marriage as you are for it, please make sure there aren't other things going on besides he's just not that into the institution.

•149•

The Age-old "He's Just Not Ready" Excuse

I'm not ready. This is the most often used excuse in the world, but it always seems to do the trick. Women love waiting around for men to be ready.

Listen, we all know that couple who's been dating for five years . . . eight years and still hasn't gotten married. We know it never works out well for that couple. So how about you stop waiting—and start looking for that guy who can't wait to love you.

150

It's a really big deal for a good guy to finally meet the woman he wants to spend the rest of his life with. Chances are, if he truly knows it, he's not going to immediately tell her that the idea of legally spending the rest of their lives together is repugnant to him. I'm just saying.

151

What's the big, nasty, awful shame, ladies? It's okay to want to get married. And it's okay to ask someone if they see themselves being married, or if they see themselves being married to you. Let me remind you: There are many, many men out there who want to be and are getting married; that's why there are so many florists, priests, and taffetamakers out there.

152

Don't spend your time on and give your heart to any guy who makes you wonder about *anything* related to his feelings for you.

153

A lot of people think marriage is bull-shit. A lot of women, men, philosophers, anthropologists, psychologists, feminists, and scientists all think, for different reasons, that marriage is a deeply flawed, outdated institution built for failure.

But let's be clear. The question at hand is only this: Is he making lame transparent excuses about marriage to cover for the fact that he really doesn't ever see a future with you?

154

Women are smart. If they really got quiet and stopped listening to the excuses, or believing what they wanted to be true and what they hope he's really saying, and just got all centered about it, I think women would always know. They'll always know the difference between a man who truly has issues with marriage but is deeply committed to the relationship and her, and a guy who's just being a weenie.

155

If you feel that he's always holding something back, or that you're spending a lot of energy trying to change yourself into something you think will make him happier, then divorce yourself from him and move on. Don't let him make you feel stupid about wanting to feel loved.

156

One hundred percent of the guys polled told us they would have no problem marrying a woman whom they were positive was the love of their life. One man answered, "What kind of knuckle-head has a problem marrying the love of his life?"

157

"Doesn't want to get married" and "Doesn't want to get married to me" are very different things. Be sure about which category he falls under.

158

If you have different views about marriage, what else are you not on the same page about? Time to take inventory.

159

If you don't feel like you're rushing, why are you waiting?

160

There's a guy out there who wants to marry you.

°161°

Please write down how long it took you to start thinking that you might want to marry the guy you're dating.

Write down how long it took you to know for sure.

Look and see if these seemed like a reasonably appropriate amount of time. Then tell yourself that he has no good excuse for not having figured that out by now too.

162

He's just not that into you if he's breaking up with you. "I don't want to go out
with you" means just that.

163

Everyone wants to be loved and needed, particularly by the person who just broke up with us.

• 164 •

The "But He Misses Me"
Excuse

Don't be flattered that he misses you. He *should* miss you. You're deeply missable. However, he's still the same person who just broke up with you. Remember, the only reason he can miss you is because he's choosing, every day, not to be with you.

$\overset{\bullet}{\underset{\bullet}{\bullet}}165\overset{\bullet}{\underset{\bullet}{\bullet}}$

The "But it Really Takes the Pressure Off Us" Excuse

It's very tempting when you really want to be with someone to settle for much, much less—even a vague, pathetic facsimile of less—than you would have ever imagined. Ladies, please, keep your eye on the prize. Remember always what you set out to get, and please don't settle for less.

166

The "But Everyone Is Doing it" Excuse

Don't underestimate the power of sex, even with someone you've been doing it with for a very long time. Especially with someone you've been doing it with for a very long time. Breaking up means not seeing them again, which also implies not seeing them naked again.

167

It's still called breakup sex. No one has yet to rename it oh-my-God-the-sex-was-so-good-we-got-back-together-again-and-lived-happily-ever-after sex.

•168•

The "But Then He Wants To Get Back Together" Excuse

This is what that guy is doing during your relationship recess: He's sniffing around for something better, and when he doesn't find it, he gets lonely and comes "home." It's not that he's so into you. It's that he's so not into being alone.

169

Deciding to get back together with someone is a complicated and difficult decision. Just remember that the person you are getting back together with is the same person who, not long before, looked you in your beautiful face, took full stock of you and all your qualities, and told you that he was no longer in need of your company.

170

The "But I'm So Damn Nice" Excuse

Don't confuse being classy with being a doormat. Classy is walking away with your head held high, graciously, and with dignity. Being a doormat is offering to drive him to the dentist for his root canal.

171

The "I Do Not Accept His Breakup" Excuse

One simple rule, ladies: Always be classy. Never be crazy. Okay, actually it's two simple rules, but trust me, you will never be sad you followed them. If for no other reason, it will ensure that you never have that awful memory of cutting his clothes in half or dumping his dog on the side of the road.

172

A guy says he doesn't want to be with you. Sometimes that guy realizes he's made the biggest mistake of his life. And then sometimes he doesn't. Either way, *either way*, your only job is to move on with your life, and fast.

173

Breakups are supposed to be just that. Breaks. Hard, clean breaks. No talking, no seeing, no touching . . . keep your hands to yourself. The relationship is over.

174

I know a couple who dated for many years and then broke up. They had a lot of mutual friends and everyone took it very hard. Five years later, they got back together again and are now happily married. During the time apart, there were no dates or phone calls or being chums. They didn't torture, confuse, or hurt each other in the process. They moved on with their lives, grew up separately, and only then realized, much later, that they could be together again.

175

One hundred percent of men polled said that when they broke up with someone, it always meant that they didn't want to go out with them anymore.

(One guy even asked, "How can you have great breakup sex if you don't break up?" Don't go out with this guy!)

176

You can't talk your way out of a breakup.
It is not up for discussion. A breakup is a
definitive action, not a democratic one.

177

Breakup sex still means you're broken up.

178

Cut him off. Let him miss you.

179

He doesn't need to be reminded that you're great.

180

He can take care of his cat.

181

"Classy" doesn't "break into his answering machine."

182

There's a guy out there who's going to be really happy that you didn't get back together with your crappy ex-boyfriend.

183

He's just not that into you if he's disappeared on you. Sometimes you have to
get closure all by yourself.

184

He's gone. Poof. Vanished into thin air. Well, there's no mixed message here. He's made it clear that he's so not into you that he couldn't even bother to leave you a Post-it.

185

The "Maybe He's Dead" Excuse

If you want to write him and ask him again to close the door in your face, for the .0001% chance his phone died and his e-mail crashed, and he lost all your contact information, be my guest. Just don't say I didn't warn you.

186

There's nothing worse than having no answer, in business, friendships, and especially romantic relationships. But the bad news is, no answer is your answer. He may not have written you a good-bye note, but his silence is a deafening "see you later."

●·187●

The "But Can't I at Least Yell at Him?" Excuse

In the short term it might feel good to call someone and yell at him. But in the long run, you will have wished that you had not given him that much credit for ruining your life. Or even your day.

188

The "But I Just Want an Answer" Excuse

Do you deserve to know what happened? Yes. But fortunately for you, I can tell you what happened. You were dating *the worst person in the world*.

Nothing he could possibly say will be satisfying to you. But what will be satisfying is if you don't spend another moment of your energy on him.

189

Sometimes a person's behavior is so abhorrent that it leaves little doubt as to what to do. The big mistake you made was choosing that person to begin with. The quickest way to rectify that mistake is by learning from that, moving on, and choosing much more wisely in the future. And quick, before any more of your precious time is wasted.

190

The reason it's so painful when some-one disappears is you have to face the fact that the person you loved had probably left you a long time before he grabbed his coat and scrammed.

191

Don't ask yourself what you did wrong or how you could have done it differently. Don't waste your valuable heart and mind trying to figure out why he did what he did. Or thinking back on all the things he said, and wondering what was the truth and what was the lie. The only thing you need to know is that it's really good news: He's gone. Hallelujah.

192

There's nothing worse, in dating terms, *nothing worse*, than that sick feeling you get in the pit of your stomach when it looks like the guy you were seeing or getting to know has decided to bail on you instead of talking to you about it. *Nothing worse.*

193

Breakups are horrible. But to me, what's truly devastating is to feel like you weren't even worth a breakup. It's natural to want to do something about that.

But I guess the hope is that when a guy no longer wants to communicate with me, and doesn't have the manners or courage to tell me that to my face, he's given me all the information I need. It's the toughest one of all to put into practice.

194

One hundred percent of men polled who had "disappeared" on a woman said that at the time they were completely aware of what a horrible thing they were doing, and no woman calling them up and talking to them would have changed that.

195

He might be lying in the hospital with amnesia, but more likely he's just not that into you.

196

No answer is your answer.

197

Don't give him the chance to reject you again.

198

Let his mother yell at him. You're too busy.

199

There's no mystery—he's gone and he wasn't good enough for you.

200

He's just not that into you if he's married (and other insane variations of being unavailable). If you're not able to love freely, it's not really love.

201

This is going to be controversial, but I am going to say it anyway. No matter how powerful and real your feelings may be for someone, if that person cannot fully and honestly return them and therefore actively love you back, these feelings mean nothing.

202

The "But His Wife Is Such a Bitch" Excuse

Regardless of how much his marriage sucks or how awful his wife is to him, it obviously isn't that bad or he would get out of it. A good relationship should not be lived in secrecy. Go find yourself one worth living out loud.

• 203 •

I know things seem a lot easier when your affair is with a man whose wife is an evil, shrieking, insulting hag. No matter what their relationship or circumstances are, you are still helping a man cheat on his wife. Let's agree you're better than that.

204

The "But He's Really a Good Person" Excuse

This is no joke, and I'm not even going to try to be glib. You want love and you want to be loved and you think you've finally found it. But he's married. Please try not to ignore that fact. He's married to someone else. I know you're different, and it's different, but the fact is, he's still married. If there's only one red flag you are unable to ignore in your entire life, please make it this one. There's simply too much at stake for everyone involved.

•205•

The "I Should Wait it Out" Excuse

It's never going to be good news if you have to think of your relationship in terms of "waiting for him." He's not a stock you're supposed to be investing in. He's a man who's supposed to be emotionally available enough to talk to you, see you, and perhaps fall madly in love with you.

206

Yes. You are going to meet many men in many different stages of recovering from relationships. If he is really into you, he will get over his issues fast and make sure he doesn't lose you. Or he will make it clear to you how he feels, so there's no mystery, and tell you up front that he's not up to it right now. And then you can best be sure, the minute he is ready, he will run out and find you. *You are not easily forgettable.*

207

I have to be honest—it feels really noble and romantic and dramatic to be filled with longing and heartache, knowing the man you love, for whatever reason, can't be yours right now. And you're willing to wait for him, because your feelings for him are so very large and profound. If you're really comfortable with that, too, and nothing that this book or your friends or your therapist can say will help you change that, then eventually, I hope, like me, you'll just get tired of it.

208

My friend met a guy who had just broken up with his girlfriend two weeks before, after living with her for three years. She thought that she was just going to be his "rebound" romance. He thought she may be that as well. But even though he could have used the excuse that he wasn't ready yet, because he had "just gotten out of something," he didn't. Because he was really into her, he never let her feel that he wasn't available to her. They are now in a serious relationship.

209

A friend of mine was on a first date with a woman who mentioned she was also dating a married man. He immediately told her there wouldn't be a second date, because if she didn't like herself enough to be in a proper relationship, why should he?

210

He's married.

211

Unless he's all yours, he's still hers.

212

There are cool, loving, *single* men in the world. Find one of them to go out with.

213

If a guy is yelling about his ex-wife or crying over his last girlfriend, try to find someone else to take you to the movies.

214

Don't be that girl.

215

You are not easily forgotten. Let him find you when he's ready.

216

List all the things you want or have ever wanted in a man. Now look at your list. Did "married" or "emotionally unavailable" make that list?

Yeah, we didn't think so. You're far too classy and smart for that.

217

He's just not that into you if he's a selfish jerk, a bully, or a really big freak.

218

Forget about him and his good qualities. Even forget about his bad ones. Forget about all his excuses and what he promises. Ask yourself one question only: Is he making you happy?

219

People are complicated. They are a mixed bag of lovable and dysfunctional qualities. That's why they are so darn confusing. That's why trying to figure them out is a waste of time. Is he making you happy? I don't mean some of the time, on rare occasions, not that often, "but the good still outweighs the bad." Does he make it clear in his actions every day that your happiness is important to him? If the answer is no, cut him loose and go find a man with a higher "good count."

220

The "He's Really Trying to Be Better" Excuse

Try not to be four years into a relationship when it suddenly dawns on you that the guy you're with is a big, selfish jerk. Chances are, Jerk Boy has been trying to show you who he is since day one.

221

He doesn't have to love your CD collection. He doesn't have to love your shoes. But any good, mature guy better make an attempt to love your friends and family—especially when they're great.

222

There is no reason to yell at anyone ever, unless you are screaming "LOOK OUT FOR THAT BUS!" And it's not temporary. People who yell are people with anger issues who need help. People who yell are people who think they're entitled to yell. Hey, hot stuff, do you want to be that couple? You know—that couple where the guy yells at his wife all the time? Even better, do you want him to be that dad? I didn't think so.

223

There's lots of behavior that can be considered abusive that doesn't include being beaten about the head and neck. That includes getting yelled at, being publicly humiliated, or being made to feel fat and unattractive. It's hard to feel worthy of love when someone is going out of their way to make you feel worthless. Being told to get out of these relationships may not work for you. Knowing that you're better than these relationships is the place to start. You *are* better than these relationships.

224

When two people are connecting, they hunger for information about each other, a sliver of what life is like when you're not together, a glimpse into their past, a peek into their mind, all in hopes of getting under their skin.

Remember, you are the catch. They are out to snare you.

225

The "He's Just Finding Himself" Excuse

A man that's really into you and himself will try to get his act together as fast as he can. That means, first and foremost, collecting a salary.

People go through rough patches all the time. But as the saying goes, when the going gets tough, the tough don't ask to borrow five hundred bucks so they can pay their bar tab down at Paddy's. The only job you need to worry about is the job of finding yourself someone who would never be that comfortable living off of you and your family's money.

226

The "Maybe it's Just His Little Quirk" Excuse

You will meet people who don't like to be touched, or kissed, or who don't like sex. You can spend a lot of time trying to fix them, or wondering if you should take it personally. Or you can realize that they simply don't like to do the things you find absolutely essential to your enjoyment of life, and then go find yourself someone who does.

227

If you date, you will meet your share of weirdos and jerks. That is as sure as death and taxes. The only thing in your control is how long you allow these gentlemen to take up space in your life. In case you're not sure, it should be about ten minutes from when they first display their completely unacceptable behavior (or lizardlike tail). Ten minutes still gives you time to put on all your clothes and make sure you have deleted your number from his cell phone.

228

There's a difference between eccentric and insane. "Eccentric" will sometimes wear a velvet jacket. "Insane" will only have sex with you when wearing it. There's a difference between teasing and abuse. Teasing is "Björk called. She wants her dress back." Abuse is "Boy, are you getting *fat*." But the biggest difference is you. You are ultimately better than the treatment you are receiving from these men.

229

Being lonely, being alone, for many people, sucks. I get it, I get it, I get it. But still I have to say that, yes, my true belief is that being with somebody who makes you feel shitty or doesn't honor the person you are, is worse.

230

The statistics are bleak. But don't use statistics to keep you down or keep you frightened. You can't do anything with these statistics except scare yourself and your girlfriends. So I say, "Fuck statistics." It's your life—how dare you not have faith in it! The only story that has ever helped me live my life successfully is the story of faith; I believe that life will turn out well. More fervently, I believe that you have no other choice than to believe that.

231

We are all tired of operating from a place of fear. You want to believe that you are better than all the crap you've been taking from all these men all these years. Well, you are.

232

You are an excellent, foxy human being worthy of love, and the only way you can pursue that idea is by honoring yourself. At the very least this means ridding your world of dudes who are not worthy and setting a standard of excellence in your daily life.

233

Let's start with this statistic: You are delicious. Be brave, my sweet. I know you can get lonely. I know you can crave companionship and sex and love so badly that it physically hurts. But I truly believe that the only way you can find out that there's something better out there is to first *believe* there's something better out there. I'll believe it for you until you're ready.

234

A guy friend of mine refuses to break up with a woman he's engaged to because he's scared. (Yes, we're a classy species.) When I beg the guy to pull the plug, he always says the same thing: "I'm waiting for the big fight. I'm just waiting for the big fight." In the meantime, he picks on, bickers with, needles his fiancée, just so he can have the "big fight" and get it over with. It's not pretty, but I hope it scares you just a bit.

235

One hundred percent of the guys polled said they have never tried to torture or humiliate a girl they were really into. Well, that's a start.

236

Life is hard enough as it is without choosing someone difficult to share it with.

237

You deserve to be with someone who is nice to you all the time. (You have to be nice to them, too.)

238

There's never a reason to shout at someone unless they are in imminent danger.

239

Freaks should remain at the circus, not in your apartment.

240

You already have one asshole. You don't need another.

241

Make a space in your life for the glorious things you deserve.

242

Have faith. What other choice is there?

243

Sure. There are the stories. Guys that get pursued by some girl first and she ends up being the love of his life; the guy that treats this girl that he sometimes sleeps with like shit for a couple of years, but she keeps at him and now he's a devoted husband and father; the guy who doesn't call a girl that he's slept with for a month, and then calls her and they live happily ever after; the woman who is sleeping with the married guy who she ends up marrying and having a blissful long-term marriage with.

We don't want you to listen to these stories. These stories don't help you.

These stories are the exceptions to the rule. We want you to think of yourself as the rule.

244

Thinking of yourself as the exception is what got you into this mess in the first place. Tell your friends to stop telling you these stories. Whenever you hear one of these stories, a story where some woman was treated badly but it all worked out okay in the end, just put your hands up to your ears and go "la-la-la-la-la!"

245

You are exceptional, but not the exception!!

246

It seems like it's our duty to discuss what one must do *after* the breakup. We're not psychiatrists or very girly, so we're not going to talk about candles and bubble baths and sending yourself flowers. But I think we could ask you to at least try to notice, even just a tiny bit, how good it feels to be out of a relationship with someone who actually wasn't that into you. Can you at least feel that sense of relief?

247

When you think about it, making all those excuses for someone and trying to "figure someone out" takes up a lot of energy. Think of all the time you've opened up for so many other more positive things besides obsessing over *him*.

248

Yes, breakups are painful, even from someone you may have only dated a few times. You may have been really excited about him and had a lot of hopes for the future. But how empowering to have the mental clarity to say, "He just wasn't that into me." Can you imagine that girl in the future? Nothing will be able to stop her!

Now, there's a million things you can do after a breakup; what you do during that time—yoga, affirmation tapes, murder—is your business. But basically you're going to have to feel the pain, you're going to have to go through it, and then you're going to have to get over it. All we can try to do in this book is help you do it differently in the future. The first thing we're going to recommend is setting some standards.

250

Sure, you say, "But I have standards."
Well, your standards led you to this
book, so let's raise them. Let's set a dig-
nified bar for you to exist at. Let's put
you in charge of how it's going to go
next time. (But you ask, "What if there
isn't going to be a next time?" And we
say, "Stow that bad-news cargo on the
sure-to-sink ship. Because that ship is
about to hit Sad Island and we don't
want you on it.")

251

A standard is setting a level for yourself of what you will or won't tolerate. You get to decide how it's going to be for you. You can now design the person you want to be in the future, and the standards you want to have.

Make sure you know what you stand for and what you believe in.

252

I WILL NOT GO OUT WITH A
MAN WHO HASN'T ASKED ME
OUT FIRST.

253

I WILL NOT GO OUT WITH A
MAN WHO KEEPS ME WAITING
BY THE PHONE.

254

I WILL NOT DATE A MAN WHO
ISN'T SURE HE WANTS TO DATE
ME.

255

I WILL NOT DATE A MAN WHO MAKES ME FEEL SEXUALLY UNDESIRABLE.

256

I WILL NOT DATE A MAN WHO
DRINKS OR DOES DRUGS TO
AN EXTENT THAT MAKES ME
UNCOMFORTABLE.

257

I WILL NOT BE WITH A MAN
WHO'S AFRAID TO TALK ABOUT
OUR FUTURE.

258

I WILL NOT, UNDER ANY CIRCUM-
STANCES, SPEND MY PRECIOUS
TIME WITH A MAN WHO HAS
ALREADY REJECTED ME.

259

I WILL NOT DATE A MAN WHO IS
MARRIED.

260

I WILL NOT BE WITH A MAN WHO
IS NOT CLEARLY A GOOD, KIND,
LOVING PERSON.

261

Now it's your turn. Only you know the standards you haven't set for yourself. Don't forget them.

262

MY SUPER-HELPFUL STANDARDS
THAT I WILL NEVER EVER FOR-
GET OR FORSAKE NO MATTER
HOW HOT I THINK HE IS:

1.
2.
3.
4.
5.

263

Seriously, are you really sure I can't ask the guy out? Guys say I'm intimidating. I should be allowed to help them out a bit.

Most of the great things we want in life are intimidating. That's what makes life so darn exciting. Do you really have time for a guy who's so afraid of you that he's not even capable of inviting you for coffee?

264

Are you so sure there are so many great guys out there, that I can just throw all these other less-than-perfect guys away?

I don't know how to answer that except to say that being in a good relationship is much better than being in a bad relationship, and you'll never be able to be in a good relationship if you're sticking with Mr. Shitty What's His Name. Only you can know if the relationship you're in isn't good enough for you. A good indication that it's not is if you're only staying with What's His Name because you're scared.

265

What if I would rather be with someone who might not be that into me than be alone?

I get it. You can feel like crap and be alone. Or feel like crap and at least have someone to spend the holidays with. Got it. It seems like it might be a fair trade, except for the fact that it means the only two options you are giving yourself involve feeling like crap. By staying with the guy who's not that into you, you are ensuring that you're never going to find one that is. I say, not to anyone's surprise, take the risk of not having someone to spend Christmas with, possibly feel lonely for a while, but know that you're doing it for a much bigger payoff at the end.

266

Do you really think there are that many men out there who are capable of being as loving as you think I deserve?

Yes. I do. I do. I do. Otherwise I wouldn't be writing this book.

267

You say that I shouldn't talk to my ex-boyfriend unless he's begging to get back together with me. But then you also say that I should be suspicious of a guy that wants to get back together with me after he's broken up with me. What's up?

Well, my first point was, I want you to see the difference between an ex who just misses you and needs a fix, and a man who realizes he made a mistake and seriously wants to get back together with you. But even then, I think you must proceed with caution and truly question this man's motives. And I definitely want you to stay away from any man that keeps breaking up with you on a regular basis.

268

Do you think a bad guy can change into a good guy, within a relationship?

I'm loath to say this to someone who might be coming from an unhappy situation and is wanting me to validate it. I believe that anything is possible. However, my experience has been that most men do not change, and the ones I've seen change only changed when they met new women.

What if I only seem to be attracted to guys who are just not that into me?

Okay, so you have this crazy quirk that somehow makes you able to sniff out the men that are going to end up being emotionally unavailable to you. We can talk about why that is and what your priorities are that make these men seem attractive to you. However, what we can most quickly rectify is how long you stick around once you know that he's just not that into you. A lot of guys, good and bad, are going to fly in your direction. Which ones you pick to invest your time in is where you have your control. Immediately.

C'mon, admit it. Sometimes there are real, sincere reasons why a guy who really likes me isn't able to get in a serious relationship with me. It doesn't have to mean he's just not that into me.

Maybe there are men like that out there, maybe there aren't. This is the only thing you need to remember: Mr. I'm Just Not Up For It is exactly the same guy as Mr. I'm Just Not That Into You. Both guys don't want to be with you. One of them may say he can't be with you, but it's still the same result. He isn't going to be with you. Don't let his personal complications confuse you into waiting around for him. He's not able to be really into you. And you deserve better.

271

The "he's just not that into you" concept can truly have a magical transcendent effect. It's not bad news if it helps you free yourself from a relationship that is beneath you. And we both know that only you can free yourself. I don't pretend to know how to fix you. I do know how to help you recognize the problem. I do know that you are worthy of having great relationships and an even better life. I do think you are beautiful and somewhere deep down inside you know it too, otherwise you wouldn't be here. I believe life is a speedy and awesome gift, so don't waste the pretty.

272

If you are reading this, *you* want something better. If you are reading this, I want something better for you too.

273

I hope this book was helpful to you. I hope it made you laugh a little, in recognition. And I hope you find fantastic, healthy, life-changing love, just the way you had imagined it.

With perhaps a few surprises thrown in just for fun.

About the Authors

Comedian **Greg Behrendt** was a consultant for three consecutive seasons on *Sex and the City*. His acclaimed stand-up comedy has been seen on HBO, *Comedy Central Presents . . .* , *The Tonight Show with Jay Leno*, *Late Show with David Letterman*, and *Late Night with Conan O'Brien*. He lives in Los Angeles with his wife and daughter.

Liz Tuccillo was an executive story editor of HBO's Emmy-winning *Sex and the City* and has also written for Off Broadway. She is currently living and dating in New York City.

Find the *complete* truth inside the book
that sparked a dating revolution.

GREG BEHRENDT & LIZ TUCCILLO

he's just notthat into you

the no-excuses truth to understanding guys

FROM A WRITER AND A CONSULTANT OF
Sex and the City

Now available from HarperElement

ISBN: 0-00-719821-3